CHRISTMAS AT HOME

Dessert Lover's COOKBOOK

HOLIDAY RECIPES & MORE

BARBOUR
PUBLISHING

Carrie Brown

© 2008 by Barbour Publishing, Inc.

Compiled by Carrie Brown.

ISBN 978-1-60260-160-4

Published by Barbour Publishing, Inc., P.O. Box 719, Uhrichsville, Ohio 44683, www.barbourbooks.com

Our mission is to publish and distribute inspirational products offering exceptional value and biblical encouragement to the masses.

 Member of the
Evangelical Christian
Publishers Association

Printed in China.

Mini Peanut Butter Cheesecakes

(FROM THE KITCHEN OF REBECCA VAN ZANT BAHUN)

2 (8 ounce) packages cream cheese,
  softened
¾ cup sugar
2 eggs

1 teaspoon vanilla
1 box vanilla wafers
24 chocolate peanut butter cups

Preheat oven to 350 degrees. In bowl, beat cream cheese, sugar, eggs, and vanilla until well mixed and smooth. Place 1 vanilla wafer in each cup of mini cupcake tin. Fill each cup about halfway with cheesecake mixture. Push 1 peanut butter cup into center of each cheesecake. Bake for 15 minutes. Run knife around sides of each cheesecake and allow to cool completely before removing from tin.

Monkey Bread

¾ cup sugar   ½ cup butter, melted
2 tablespoons cinnamon   ¾ cup finely chopped pecans
2 tubes refrigerated biscuits, cut into quarters

Preheat oven to 350 degrees. Mix sugar and cinnamon in resealable plastic bag. Toss
biscuit pieces, a few at a time, in sugar mixture until well coated. Place biscuits in
greased Bundt pan. Add remaining sugar-cinnamon mixture and pecans to butter
and heat until sugar is dissolved. Pour evenly over biscuits. Bake for 25 minutes. Let
cool until warm. Invert cake pan on round platter. You can separate monkey bread
into individual servings or guests can pull off pieces of bread.

Contents

INDEX

Drinkable Desserts

Blessed is the season which engages the whole
world in a conspiracy of love.

HAMILTON WRIGHT MABIE

Truffle Mugs

4 cups very hot, strong coffee
8 dark chocolate truffles,
   cut into quarters

Whipped cream for garnish

Pour coffee into 4 festive mugs and place truffle pieces in bowl. Spoon whipped cream into serving dish. Serve coffee to your guests and invite them to stir truffle pieces into their coffee. Coffee should be stirred constantly until truffles have melted. Guests can garnish their drinks with whipped cream if desired.

Peppermint Iced Coffee

Ice
¾ cup strong coffee

Peppermint coffee syrup
Skim milk or half-and-half

Fill large glass with ice. In large mug, mix coffee and peppermint coffee syrup. Start with 1 teaspoon of syrup and add more to taste. Pour coffee mixture over ice and stir to start melting process. Add milk or half-and-half as desired.

Basic Hot Chocolate Mix

4 cups powdered chocolate milk mix

9½ cups powdered milk

1¾ cups coffee creamer

1 cup powdered sugar

Mix all ingredients together and store in airtight container. Use ⅓ cup mix to 6-ounce mug of hot water. Serve with marshmallows or Homemade Marshmallows (see page 14).

Minty Hot Chocolate

4 cups boiling water
1⅓ cups Basic Hot Chocolate
   Mix (see page 10)
¼ to ½ teaspoon peppermint
   extract, according to taste

4 candy canes
Homemade Marshmallows
(see page 14)

Mix water, hot chocolate mix, and extract. Pour into 4 mugs. Serve each with a candy cane for stirring and Homemade Marshmallows.

But the angel said to them,
"Do not be afraid. I bring you good news of
great joy that will be for all the people.
Today in the town of David a Savior has been
born to you; he is Christ the Lord.

LUKE 2:10–11

Mexican Hot Cocoa

3 cups water
1⅓ cups Basic Hot Chocolate
    Mix (see page 10)
½ teaspoon cinnamon
1 teaspoon vanilla

Whipped cream for garnish
4 cinnamon sticks for stirring

Combine water, hot chocolate mix, cinnamon, and vanilla in blender. Mix on medium for 30 seconds or until well blended. Pour into saucepan and heat until almost boiling. Pour into 4 mugs and garnish with a dollop of whipped cream and a cinnamon stick.

Homemade Marshmallows

(From the Kitchen of Lee-Ann Rushton)

2 tablespoons unflavored gelatin
1½ cups water, divided
1 teaspoon vanilla or peppermint extract

2 cups sugar
Coconut or powdered sugar

Combine gelatin and ½ cup water. Allow to swell for 10 minutes. In large saucepan over low heat, heat sugar and 1 cup water, stirring constantly until sugar dissolves. Dissolve gelatin into sugar mixture and bring to a boil. Boil steadily for 15 minutes. Allow to cool until lukewarm. Beat well until very thick and white. Add vanilla or peppermint extract. Pour into large wet jelly roll pan and spread out evenly. Chill until set. Cut into squares and roll in coconut or powdered sugar. Keep chilled.

Cranberry Spiced Cider

1 quart apple cider
2 cups cranberry juice cocktail
1 orange

1 lemon
½ teaspoon whole cloves
3 cinnamon sticks

Combine all ingredients in large stockpot and simmer on stove for about 1 hour. Ladle into cups and serve.

Sweet and Tangy Tea Mix

2 cups orange drink mix
2 cups instant iced tea mix
2 cups sugar
¾ teaspoon cinnamon

¾ teaspoon ground cloves
1 teaspoon ginger
Thin orange slices for garnish

Mix all ingredients well in airtight container. Keep in a cool, dry place. To serve, put 1 tablespoon mixture in mug and add hot water. Stir well and place slice of orange on side of cup.

Wassail

2 quarts apple cider
1 cup orange juice
1 cup lemon juice
1 cup pineapple juice

1 cup sugar
1 teaspoon whole cloves
1 navel orange, cut into slices
3 cinnamon sticks

In large saucepan, combine all ingredients. Simmer for 1 hour to combine flavors.
Can be frozen.

Eggnog

6 eggs, separated, room temperature
1 quart heavy cream
¼ teaspoon nutmeg plus
   extra for garnish

¾ cup sugar
½ teaspoon vanilla

Beat egg yolks with about half the sugar until creamy. In separate bowl, beat egg whites until peaks form and add other half of sugar. In another bowl, beat cream until stiff peaks form. Then fold all together with vanilla. Pour into pitcher and keep in refrigerator for at least one day. Stir well before serving.

Eggnog Punch

(FROM THE KITCHEN OF DAWN CARROLL)

2 quarts French vanilla ice cream
2 quarts Eggnog (see page 18), chilled
1 liter cream soda, chilled

1 package large candy canes
Cinnamon

Place ice cream in extra-large punch bowl. Add half the eggnog. Stir and mash mixture using potato masher until ice cream is melted and mixture is well combined. Stir in remaining eggnog. Slowly pour in cream soda, stirring to combine. Sprinkle lightly with cinnamon. Hang candy canes around punch bowl for decoration and for guests to enjoy!

Spiced Apple Cider

2 quarts apple cider
1 large orange, cut into thin
    slices with peel
¼ cup brown sugar
½ teaspoon salt

¼ teaspoon nutmeg
½ teaspoon ginger
2 cinnamon sticks

In large saucepan, combine all ingredients and heat to almost boiling. Allow to cook for at least 30 minutes before serving. Serve with Christmas cookies.

Party Desserts

For centuries men have kept an appointment with Christmas. Christmas means fellowship, feasting, giving and receiving, a time of good cheer, home.

W. J. RONALD TUCKER

Fudgy Pecan Pie

2 squares semisweet chocolate
¼ cup butter
1 (14 ounce) can sweetened
  condensed milk
½ cup hot water
2 eggs, well beaten

1¼ cups pecan pieces
1 teaspoon vanilla
¼ teaspoon salt
1 unbaked piecrust

Preheat oven to 350 degrees. In saucepan over low heat, melt chocolate and butter. Stir in milk, hot water, and eggs; mix well. Remove from heat; stir in pecans, vanilla, and salt. Pour into piecrust. Bake for 40 minutes or until center is set. Cool on wire rack. Serve pie warm or chilled. Store covered in refrigerator.

Chocolate Fondue

3 milk chocolate bars
3 dark or semisweet chocolate bars
2 cups heavy cream
1 pound cake cut into cubes,
    banana slices, apple slices, strawberries,
    marshmallows, vanilla wafers, and pretzel rods for dipping

In saucepan, heat cream until almost boiling. Remove from heat and add chocolate in pieces. Stir mixture until melted. Pour into fondue pot and serve with fondue forks or bamboo skewers. Arrange the items to be dipped on a platter.

DeMarco Gallery Christmas Yule Log Cake

(FROM THE KITCHEN OF SANDRA SWEENY SILVER)

2 pints whipping cream
½ cup powdered sugar
10 to 12 thick (¼ inch to ½ inch thick,
   2 inches in diameter) chocolate
   cookies (gingerbread or chocolate
   chip cookies will also work)

½ pint heavy cream
Grated chocolate

Whip whipping cream until stiff peaks form and add sugar to sweeten. Pour heavy cream into a bowl. You will be soaking the cookies in the heavy cream as you assemble the cake. Soak one cookie in heavy cream until soft but not too soggy to handle. Prop first cookie up on the far left side of a serving platter. Spread a layer of whipped cream on the cookie and then put the second soaked cookie next to it to create a sandwich. Continue this whipped cream and cookie order until you reach the other side of the platter or the desired length. When the log is as long as you want it, cover entire Yule log with whipped cream. Chill for several hours. Before serving, sprinkle log with grated chocolate.

New Year's Scottish Biscuit Cake

(FROM THE KITCHEN OF SANDRA SWEENY SILVER)

8 squares bittersweet chocolate
2 cups butter or margarine
4 eggs
4 tablespoons sugar
Pinch instant coffee

Handful chopped walnuts
(optional)
1 box vanilla wafers

In large pan, melt chocolate and butter; remove from heat. In bowl, beat together eggs, sugar, and coffee. Add small amount of chocolate mixture to egg mixture and mix quickly to temper. Add remaining chocolate mixture and nuts. Break up wafers and add to other ingredients. Spread biscuit mixture into 9x13-inch cake pan and refrigerate for at least 2 hours before serving.

Maple Glazed Nuts

(FROM THE KITCHEN OF BARBARA BAHUN)

½ cup maple syrup
1 teaspoon cinnamon
1 teaspoon butter

1½ teaspoons pure vanilla
2 cups nuts of your choice

In iron skillet, stir together syrup, cinnamon, and butter. Cook and stir over medium heat until mixture becomes brown and thick. Add vanilla and nuts; toss to coat nuts evenly. Cool on waxed paper.

Christmas Twists

1 cup sour cream
2 tablespoons shortening
3 tablespoons sugar
⅛ teaspoon baking soda
1 teaspoon salt
1 large egg
1 package yeast

3 cups flour, sifted
2 tablespoons butter, softened
¼ cup packed brown sugar
1 teaspoon cinnamon
Red and green sugar for
    decorating

In saucepan, bring sour cream to a boil. Remove from heat and add shortening, sugar, baking soda, and salt. Mix well and allow to cool. Add egg and yeast, stirring until yeast is dissolved. Mix in flour with wooden spoon. Lightly flour cutting board. Knead dough lightly on board until smooth ball is formed. Cover with damp cloth and let stand for 5 minutes to set. Roll dough to ½-inch thickness in a 6x24-inch rectangle. Spread surface with softened butter. Mix together brown sugar and cinnamon. Sprinkle half the dough with sugar mixture down long side of rectangle. Fold unsugared half of dough over sugared half, pressing top lightly to seal. With sharp knife, cut dough into 24 1-inch strips. Take each strip of dough at both ends and twist it twice. Place on greased baking sheet. Cover with damp cloth and let rise at room temperature until very light (about 1½ hours). Right before baking, sprinkle with red and green sugar. Bake for 12 to 15 minutes at 375 degres.

Cheese and Fruit Platter #1

Concord grapes
Brie, Gouda, Edam, or Swiss cheese
Saltine crackers

Place grapes in center of large platter. Arrange cheese on one side of platter. Arrange crackers on other side of platter.

Cheese and Fruit Platter #2

Your favorite red apples, cut into crescents
Camembert, Liederkranz, or Vermont cheddar cheese
Gingersnaps
Whole mixed nuts

Place gingersnaps in center of large platter. Arrange apples and cheese around cookies (one slice apple, one slice cheese, one slice apple, etc.). Sprinkle outside of platter with mixed nuts.

Cheese and Fruit Platter #3

Cream cheese
Currant preserves
Fresh ripe pears, cut into quarters
Mini baking powder biscuits, warmed and buttered

Place cream cheese in middle of large platter. Spoon currant preserves around cheese. Arrange pears on one side of platter and biscuits on other side.

Cheese and Fruit Platter #4

Cream cheese
½ cup powdered sugar
¼ teaspoon rum flavoring
Fresh strawberries with stems

Mix cream cheese, sugar, and rum flavoring until smooth. Serve in glass bowl on large platter. Arrange strawberries around cream cheese dip.

Cheese and Fruit Platter #5

Flame Tokay grapes
Mild Wisconsin cheddar cheese
Pumpernickel bread, thinly sliced

Arrange grapes on left side of large platter. Fan out slices of Wisconsin cheddar in middle of platter. Arrange bread on right side of platter.

Cheese and Fruit Platter #6

Fresh pineapple, chunked
Sharp New York cheddar cheese
Whole wheat crackers

Place pineapple chunks in medium glass bowl. Put bowl in middle of large platter.
Arrange cheese on one side of bowl and crackers on other side.

Cheese and Fruit Platter #7

Assorted fruit (apples, pears, peaches, figs)
Candied ginger strips
Triple cream Brie
Crackers of your choice

Stew fruit in water with candied ginger strips until just tender. Strain fruit and remove ginger pieces. Chill fruit. Serve in medium serving bowl. Warm Brie according to package instructions. Place on platter with crackers and serve with fruit.

Strawberry Mousse

(FROM THE KITCHEN OF SANDRA SWEENY SILVER)

2 (10 ounce) boxes frozen strawberries,
   thawed and mashed
4 tablespoons sugar
1 envelope unflavored gelatin
Christmas sprinkles (optional)

1 pint whipping cream, whipped
Finely chopped nuts (optional)
¼ cup cold water

Add sugar to thawed, mashed strawberries. Stir and set aside. In small double boiler, mix gelatin and water. Heat until gelatin is completely dissolved. Fold gelatin into strawberries. Chill until mixture begins to thicken. Fold in whipped cream. Spoon into plastic or glass serving bowls and chill until firm. Serve with additional whipped cream, finely chopped nuts, and/or Christmas sprinkles.

Snowy Grapes

(From the Kitchen of Sandra Sweeny Silver)

1 large bunch or 2 medium bunches firm, seedless green grapes
1 (16 ounce) container sour cream
½ cup brown sugar

Pull stems off grapes and place grapes in large serving bowl. Mix in sour cream. Sprinkle brown sugar over top.

Strawberries Dipped in Chocolate

6 squares white chocolate
6 squares milk chocolate
15 large strawberries with stems on
Finely chopped nuts
Flaked coconut

Melt chocolate in microwave. Holding strawberries by stems, dip in chocolate. You can experiment with dipping in one color and then another. Place strawberries on tray or cookie sheet lined with waxed paper. After a few minutes, drizzle with contrast color of chocolate or sprinkle with finely chopped nuts or flaked coconut.

Apricots Dipped in Chocolate

3 squares white chocolate
3 squares milk chocolate
20 dried apricots

Melt chocolate in microwave. Holding apricots by one end, dip in chocolate halfway. Place on tray or cookie sheet lined with waxed paper. Allow to cool. Arrange apricots on platter and serve.

Cranberry Parfaits

Cranberry layer:
1 bag whole cranberries,
   sweetened
2 oranges, not peeled
2 golden delicious apples,
   cored, not peeled
½ to ¾ cup honey

Additional layers:
Large container vanilla yogurt
2 cups granola of choice

Grind cranberries in food processor and put in bowl. Cut oranges into 1½-inch pieces then grind in processor. Do the same with apples. Mix fruit spread well. Add honey ¼ cup at a time. Continue adding honey until desired sweetness is reached. Layer cranberry mixture in bottom of 4 to 6 parfait glasses. Spread with vanilla yogurt and sprinkle with granola. Repeat layers until parfait glasses are full.

Cheesecake Cookies

(FROM THE KITCHEN OF BARBARA BAHUN)

Crust:
1 cup flour
⅓ cup sugar
⅓ cup butter
½ cup chopped walnuts (optional)

Filling:
1 (8 ounce) package cream cheese
¼ cup sugar
1 egg
½ teaspoon vanilla
2 tablespoons milk
1 tablespoon lemon juice (optional)

Preheat oven to 350 degrees. Blend flour, sugar, and butter with pastry cutter. Mix in nuts if desired. Reserve ½ cup of mixture for topping. Press remainder of mixture into 8x8-inch pan. Bake for 12 to 15 minutes. Soften cream cheese with spoon and blend in sugar. Add remaining ingredients and beat well. Spread over crust. Sprinkle with reserved topping. Bake for 25 minutes. Cool and cut into squares. Refrigerate before serving. Garnish with strawberry sundae topping or drizzle with chocolate sauce if desired.

Mini Strawberry Streusel Cakes

2 cups flour
1 tablespoon baking powder
½ teaspoon salt
1 cup strawberries, chopped
⅓ cup sugar
½ cup whipping cream
1 egg, lightly beaten
½ teaspoon vanilla
¼ cup butter or margarine, melted

Topping:
⅓ cup flour
¼ cup sugar
2 tablespoons butter
½ teaspoon cinnamon

Preheat oven to 400 degrees. Grease 12-cup muffin pan or use paper liners. In large bowl, combine flour, baking powder, and salt. In medium bowl, toss strawberries with sugar. Let stand for 5 minutes. Stir in cream, egg, and vanilla until well blended. Add strawberry mixture to flour mixture along with melted butter. Stir with fork until just blended. Divide batter evenly among muffin cups.

Topping: Combine flour, sugar, butter, and cinnamon with fork until mixture comes together in large crumbs. Sprinkle topping on cakes. Bake for 12 to 15 minutes until wooden toothpick comes out clean. Cool on wire rack before removing from pan.

Snowball Candy

½ cup butter
2 tablespoons milk
¾ cup honey
1 cup flour

¼ teaspoon salt
1 teaspoon vanilla
2 cups flaked coconut, divided
2 cups rice cereal

In medium saucepan, melt butter and add milk, honey, flour, and salt. Stir constantly until mixture forms ball. Remove from heat. Stir in vanilla, 1½ cups coconut, and rice cereal. Shape into 1-inch balls and roll in remaining coconut. Refrigerate. Makes about 3 dozen.

Desserts to Impress

Love came down at Christmas,
Love all lovely, Love Divine;
Love was born at Christmas;
Star and angels gave the sign.

CHRISTINA ROSSETTI

Elf Pie

4 eggs
¼ cup sugar
2 cups milk
½ cup flour
⅓ cup butter

1 cup flaked coconut
1 teaspoon vanilla
½ teaspoon nutmeg
¼ teaspoon salt
Red and green sprinkles

Preheat oven to 350 degrees. Measure all ingredients into blender. Blend on high speed for 10 seconds. Pour mixture into greased pie pan. Bake for 40 minutes or until top is brown and knife inserted in center comes out clean. Pie will separate into layers (crust, custard filling, and coconut topping) during baking. Sprinkle baked pie with red and green sprinkles.

Snow Pudding

1 tablespoon unflavored gelatin
¼ cup cold water
1 cup boiling water

1 cup sugar
¼ cup lemon juice
3 egg whites

Soak gelatin in cold water then dissolve in boiling water, adding sugar and juice. Set aside to cool and jell. Beat egg whites until stiff enough to hold shape. Put pudding in serving glasses and top with beaten egg whites.

Holiday Cherry Tartlets

1 cup graham cracker crumbs,
   finely crushed
3 tablespoons butter, melted
1 (8 ounce) package cream cheese,
   softened

1 teaspoon vanilla
1 egg
⅓ cup sugar
1 (21 ounce) can cherry pie filling

Preheat oven to 375 degrees. Grease 24 mini tartlet cups or 2 multiple tartlet pans (with approximately 2-inch cups). Mix graham cracker crumbs with butter and press mixture into bottom of cups. With electric mixer, combine cream cheese, vanilla, egg, and sugar until smooth. Fill each cup and bake for about 10 minutes. Remove from oven, cool completely, and allow to set in refrigerator overnight. Before serving, use butter knife to gently lift each tartlet out of pan. Top with small dollop of cherry pie filling. Makes 24.

Gingerbread Delight

(FROM THE KITCHEN OF SANDRA SWEENY SILVER)

1 (15 ounce) box gingerbread cake mix
½ cup butter, melted
1 cup brown sugar

1 (29 ounce) can pears, drained
Whipped cream for serving

Preheat oven to 350 degrees. Mix gingerbread cake batter according to box instructions. Pour melted butter in bottom of 9x13-inch cake pan. Sprinkle brown sugar over butter. Place pears on top of brown sugar. Pour cake batter over pears. Bake according to cake mix instructions. Allow cake to cool for several minutes. Invert onto platter. Serve with whipped cream.

Neapolitan Cupcakes

(FROM THE KITCHEN OF SARAH REID)

1½ cups flour
⅓ cup whole wheat flour
2 teaspoons baking powder
½ teaspoon baking soda
⅓ cup sugar
1 teaspoon cornstarch
6 strawberries,
   cut in half lengthwise

2 teaspoons cocoa
¼ cup semisweet chocolate chips
2 teaspoons unsalted butter
4 tablespoons sour cream, divided
1 teaspoon vanilla extract
4 tablespoons water, divided

Preheat oven to 400 degrees and grease 12 muffin cups. Whisk together flour, whole wheat flour, baking powder, baking soda, sugar, and cornstarch and divide roughly into two bowls. Stir cocoa into one of the two bowls. Melt together chocolate chips and butter; then stir in 2 tablespoons sour cream. Add chocolate mixture to cocoa muffin mix and add 2 tablespoons water. Stir gently to combine without overmixing; set aside. Add remaining 2 tablespoons sour cream, vanilla, and remaining 2 tablespoons water to plain mix and fold in gently. If either mixture is too dry, add 1 to 2 teaspoons water. Put large dollop of chocolate batter in bottom of greased cups, dividing batter evenly. Place 1 strawberry half, flat side down, on top of chocolate batter. Top with vanilla batter, again dividing batter evenly and covering chocolate batter and strawberries completely. Bake for 20 minutes. Remove from pans and cool completely on wire rack.

Pavlova

(FROM THE KITCHEN OF LEE-ANN RUSHTON)

4 jumbo egg whites, room temperature
1¼ cups superfine sugar
1 teaspoon white vinegar
1 teaspoon pure vanilla
1 tablespoon corn flour
1 pint whipping cream, whipped
Fresh strawberries and peaches, sliced
Fresh blueberries, blackberries, and raspberries

Preheat oven to 350 degrees. Beat egg whites and sugar on high speed for 10 minutes or until thick and glossy. In separate bowl, mix vinegar, vanilla, and corn flour. Add to meringue. Beat on high speed for 5 minutes. Line cookie sheet with baking paper. Draw 8-inch circle on baking paper. Spread meringue mixture evenly within the circle, making sure to leave no holes or air pockets. Smooth top. Place pavlova in oven and decrease oven temperature to 200 degrees. Bake pavlova for 1 hour. Do not open oven door during baking. Turn oven off. Open oven door slightly and leave pavlova in oven until cold. Carefully lift pavlova onto serving plate. Decorate with whipped cream and fresh fruit. Serves 10.

Candy Cane Brownies

4 eggs
2 cups sugar
1 cup butter
3 squares unsweetened chocolate
2 cups flour
1 teaspoon vanilla
1 cup crushed candy canes

Frosting:
1 pound powdered sugar
¼ teaspoon peppermint extract
Milk
Red food coloring
¼ cup water
2 tablespoons butter
½ teaspoon vanilla
2 squares unsweetened chocolate
2 cups powdered sugar

Preheat oven to 350 degrees and grease jelly roll pan. In small bowl, beat eggs; add sugar. In large saucepan, melt butter and chocolate. Cool slightly. Add sugar and egg mixture; then add flour, vanilla, and crushed candy canes. Pour into pan and bake for 20 minutes. Cool.

Frosting: Combine powdered sugar and peppermint extract with enough milk to make frosting. Mix in a few drops red food coloring. Spread over brownies. In saucepan over low heat, melt water, butter, vanilla, and chocolate. Add enough powdered sugar (up to 2 cups) to make frosting of desired consistency. Spread on top.

Cranberry-Almond Biscotti

(From the Kitchen of Lee-Ann Rushton)

1 cup dried cranberries
2 eggs
¾ cup sugar, plus extra for topping
½ cup oil
2 tablespoons finely grated orange zest
1 teaspoon cinnamon

1¼ teaspoon baking powder
1 teaspoon vanilla
½ teaspoon almond extract
¼ teaspoon salt
2 cups flour
1 cup slivered blanched almonds

Preheat oven to 350 degrees. Place cranberries in bowl of hot water and cover. Let stand for 10 minutes. Drain and set aside. In large bowl, combine eggs, ¾ cup sugar, oil, orange zest, cinnamon, baking powder, vanilla, almond extract, and salt. Whisk to blend. Add flour, almonds, and cranberries and stir until dough forms. Place dough on floured surface and knead until smooth, adding more flour if too sticky to work, about 20 turns. Divide dough in half. Continuing to work on floured surface, form each half into log about 2 inches in diameter. Carefully transfer logs to ungreased baking sheet, spacing them well apart. Sprinkle tops with sugar. Bake until golden brown and firm to the touch, about 30 minutes. Let cool for 10 minutes. Leave oven set at 350 degrees. Use spatula to transfer logs to work surface. With serrated knife, cut logs on the diagonal into ½-inch slices. Return slices cut side down to baking sheet. Bake until brown, about 20 minutes. Transfer cookies to wire racks to cool. Store in airtight container at room temperature for up to 2 weeks. Makes about 3 dozen.

Sandy's Christmas Truffles

(FROM THE KITCHEN OF SANDRA SWEENY SILVER)

3 cups semisweet chocolate chips
1 (14 ounce) can sweetened
   condensed milk
2 tablespoons butter, softened
Cocoa

Crushed nuts
Powdered sugar
Christmas sprinkles

Melt chocolate chips in double boiler. Stir in condensed milk and butter. Cook until mixture thickens. Cool until firm. Use melon baller or teaspoon to scoop small amount of truffle mixture. Roll into ball. Dip truffles in cocoa, crushed nuts, powdered sugar, or sprinkles. Allow to set before sharing.

Pretzel Wreaths

1 (16 ounce) package white or milk chocolate candy melts
Almond or peppermint extract (optional)
1 bag small pretzel twists
Christmas sprinkles

Melt chocolate, adding a few drops almond or peppermint extract if desired. Dip rounded bottoms of five pretzels into chocolate. Lay pretzels on waxed paper in a circle with sides touching and chocolate edges toward center. Repeat and place second circle on top of first, slightly staggered. Decorate wreath with sprinkles. Allow to cool completely before packaging.

Pears en Croute with Raspberry Sauce

(FROM THE KITCHEN OF BERYL KEMP)

2 (15 ounce) packages refrigerated piecrusts
5 to 6 medium firm pears, unpeeled with stems on
1 egg yolk
1 tablespoon water
1 (10 ounce) package frozen raspberries, thawed
Raw sugar for sprinkling
Spearmint or holly leaves for garnish

Unfold piecrusts one at a time. Place on lightly floured surface and roll each into 10-inch square. Cut each square into 1-inch strips. Starting at bottom of pear, carefully begin wrapping with one pastry strip, starting to spiral upward, making sure to overlap strips by ¼ inch as you cover pear. Continue wrapping by moistening ends of strips with water and joining to previous strips until pear is completely covered. Repeat with remaining pears and pastry strips. Place pears on baking sheet. Combine egg and water; brush evenly on pastry. Chill for 30 minutes in refrigerator. Puree raspberries; strain to remove seeds. Shortly before dinner, bake at 350 degrees for 1 hour or until tender. Puddle sauce on each dessert plate and place pear on top. Sprinkle with raw sugar to give pears a sparkle effect and add spearmint leaves or holly near stems.

Crème Celeste

(FROM THE KITCHEN OF SANDRA SWEENY SILVER)

3 cups heavy cream
1½ cups sugar
4½ teaspoons unflavored gelatin
9 tablespoons cold water

3 cups sour cream
Frozen red raspberries, thawed
(or fresh raspberries mashed
with lots of sugar)

In saucepan, combine heavy cream and sugar. Over medium-low heat, stir with whisk until sugar is dissolved. Soften gelatin in cold water. Whisk gelatin into cream. When gelatin is dissolved, whisk in sour cream. Stir until just blended and smooth. Pour mixture into lightly greased mold. Chill for 4 to 5 hours until firm. Remove from mold by setting it in warm water for several minutes. Then invert onto white platter. Surround with raspberries. Save a few to sprinkle on top. Serves 12 to 16.

Giftable Desserts

The magi, as you know, were wise men—
wonderfully wise men who brought gifts to the
Babe in the manger. They invented the art
of giving Christmas presents.

O. HENRY

Oatmeal-Cranberry White Chocolate Chunk Cookies

(FROM THE KITCHEN OF JACKIE BAUMGARTNER BAHUN)

⅔ cup butter
⅔ cup brown sugar
2 eggs
1 teaspoon vanilla
1½ cups flour
1 teaspoon baking soda
½ teaspoon salt

1½ cups oats
¾ cup dried cranberries
⅔ cup white chocolate chunks
⅔ cup chopped walnuts

Preheat oven to 375 degrees. In large bowl, beat butter and brown sugar until light and fluffy. Add eggs and vanilla, mixing well. Combine dry ingredients in separate bowl. Gradually add to butter mixture, mixing well. Stir in cranberries, chocolate chunks, and walnuts. Drop by rounded teaspoonfuls onto ungreased cookie sheet. Bake for 8 to 10 minutes or until golden brown.

Crisp Honey Cookies

(FROM THE KITCHEN OF BARBARA BAHUN)

½ cup honey
½ cup butter
½ teaspoon almond extract or vanilla
1¾ cup whole wheat pastry flour

1 teaspoon baking powder
2 tablespoons wheat germ or bran
1 teaspoon cinnamon

Preheat oven to 350 degrees. In large bowl, cream honey, butter, and extract. In separate bowl, combine dry ingredients and add to butter mixture. Mix well. Roll into small balls. Bake for 8 to 10 minutes.

Frosted Grapes

Large bunches of firm, seedless grapes (green or dark)
Superfine sugar

Divide grapes into small bunches of 5 to 7 grapes. Sprinkle grapes with sugar. Place bunches on cookie sheet. Refrigerate for 1 hour or more. Can be packaged in cellophane or plastic wrap. Also make a beautiful garnish for a cheese platter.

White Chocolate Truffles

1 (16 ounce) package white chocolate candy melts or chips
2/3 cup heavy cream
2 teaspoons almond extract or peppermint extract
Christmas sprinkles

In a double boiler, heat chocolate and cream, stirring until complete melted. Remove from heat and add flavoring. Pour into bowl and allow to cool in refrigerator until firm. Use melon baller or teaspoon to scoop small amount of mixture. Roll into balls, then roll in sprinkles. Place on cooking sheet covered with waxed paper. Allow truffles to set before sharing.

Peppermint Bark

1 (16 ounce) package white or dark chocolate candy melts
½ teaspoon peppermint extract
6 candy canes, crushed

Melt chocolate according to package instructions. Add extract and stir. Pour melted chocolate onto cookie sheet lined with waxed paper and spread evenly. Sprinkle candy cane pieces onto chocolate and gently press down. Refrigerate until set. Break into pieces. Store in airtight container in refrigerator.

Gingerbread Fudge

1 cup sugar
1 cup packed light brown sugar
¼ cup molasses
¼ cup light corn syrup
½ cup whipping cream
¼ teaspoon salt
½ teaspoon cream of tartar
2 tablespoons instant espresso powder
  dissolved in ¼ cup water

¾ cup dark chocolate, finely
  chopped
1 teaspoon vanilla
¼ teaspoon ginger
¾ teaspoon allspice
3 tablespoons butter

Line 8x8-inch pan with foil and grease with butter. In large saucepan, combine sugars, molasses, corn syrup, cream, salt, cream of tartar, and espresso. Cook over medium heat, stirring constantly until sugar is dissolved (3 to 4 minutes). Remove from heat; stir in chocolate until melted and smooth. Return to heat and cook without stirring until mixture reaches 238 degrees (soft ball stage). Remove from heat and stir in vanilla, spices, and butter. Allow to cool to 110 degrees. Beat until mixture loses sheen and forms peaks. Pour into prepared pan and let stand at room temperature for at least 3 hours. Lift out by corners of foil.

Butter Spritz Cookies

1 cup butter	1 teaspoon vanilla
1 cup sugar	3 cups flour
1 egg	1 teaspoon salt

Preheat oven to 350 degrees. In large bowl, cream butter and sugar on medium-high speed until light and fluffy. Mix in egg and vanilla. Add flour and salt and mix with wooden spoon until blended. Transfer dough to cookie press. Press onto ungreased baking sheet, forming 2-inch rounds. Bake until light brown and firm to the touch, about 10 minutes. Transfer to wire rack and cool.

Seven-Layer Bars

½ cup butter, melted
1 cup graham cracker crumbs
1 cup semisweet chocolate chips
1 cup butterscotch chips
1 cup chopped pecans

1 cup flaked coconut
1 (14 ounce) can sweetened
  condensed milk

Preheat oven to 350 degrees. Pour melted butter into 9x13-inch pan. Spread graham cracker crumbs over butter, pressing lightly to make crust. Sprinkle with chocolate chips, butterscotch chips, pecans, and coconut. Pour condensed milk over top. Bake for 25 minutes.

Cottage Cheese Cookies

(FROM THE KITCHEN OF BARBARA BAHUN)

1 cup butter, softened
1 cup small-curd cottage cheese
1 cup whole wheat pastry flour
1 cup unbleached white flour

¼ teaspoon baking powder
1½ cups chopped dates
½ cup water

Preheat oven to 425 degrees. In large bowl, cream butter and cottage cheese. In separate bowl, blend flours and baking powder; add to butter mixture. Shape into ball and chill for 1 hour. Meanwhile, cook dates and water until well blended. Roll out dough. Cut into squares and place scant teaspoon of cooked dates in middle of each square. Fold over one corner and seal all edges to form triangle. Bake on ungreased cookie sheet for 12 minutes. Remove from cookie sheet immediately.

Reindeer Food

10 cups crispy cereal squares
1¼ cups white chocolate chips
½ cup peanut butter

¼ cup butter
½ teaspoon vanilla
1½ cups powdered sugar

Put cereal in large bowl. In saucepan, melt chocolate chips, peanut butter, and butter. Remove from heat and add vanilla. Pour mixture over cereal and toss. Add powdered sugar to bowl and toss until cereal is well coated. Turn out on cookie sheets lined with waxed paper to cool.

Almond Butter Crunch

1½ cups coarsely chopped almonds,
   divided
½ cup butter or margarine
1½ cups sugar
1 tablespoon light corn syrup

3 tablespoons water
12 ounces melting chocolate wafers

Spread almonds on waxed paper and microwave for 7 to 10 minutes, stirring frequently until lightly toasted. Butter rimmed cookie sheet. Microwave butter in medium glass dish for 1½ to 2 minutes. Stir in sugar, corn syrup, and water. Heat for 12 to 14 minutes until mixture is color of peanut butter (soft crack stage, 270 to 290 degrees). Stir in ¾ chopped almonds. Spread evenly over prepared cookie sheet. When mixture sets up, melt half of chocolate and spread over one side. Sprinkle with remaining nuts. When hard, turn over and repeat on other side.

Chocolate Lollipops

Red-colored chocolate candy melts
Green-colored chocolate candy melts
White chocolate candy melts
Lollipop sticks
Christmas-themed lollipop molds

Melt chocolate in double boiler. Pour chocolate into lollipop molds. Tap molds against work surface to force out any air bubbles. Place lollipop sticks in far enough that they won't fall out. Allow lollipops to cool and set. Gently remove lollipops from mold. You can experiment with decorating the lollipops by "painting" contrast chocolate colors into molds before pouring in main color or by placing sprinkles in molds before adding chocolate.

Chocolate-Covered Pretzels #1

1 (16 ounce) package chocolate candy melts (dark, milk, or white)
1 large package miniature pretzels twists
Christmas sprinkles or colored sugar

Melt candy melts in double boiler, stirring constantly. One at a time, dip pretzels in chocolate with fork or small tongs, covering completely. Place on cookie sheet lined with waxed paper. Gently shake sprinkles or colored sugar over pretzels and allow to cool. Store in plastic container in a cool, dry place or freeze in airtight container.

Chocolate-Covered Pretzels #2

6 ounces dark chocolate candy melts
6 ounces milk chocolate candy melts
6 ounces white chocolate candy melts
2 large packages pretzel rods
Christmas sprinkles

Mini candy-covered
  chocolate pieces
Chopped nuts

Melt three types of chocolate in separate bowls in microwave. Dip pretzel rods in chocolate of choice and place on cookie sheet lined with waxed paper. Allow to set for a few minutes. Dip or roll each pretzel rod in topping of choice (sprinkles, candy-covered chocolate pieces, or nuts). You can also dip pretzels in dark chocolate and then drizzle with white chocolate. Use your imagination to create festive goodies.

Aunt Peg's Springerle Cookies

(FROM THE KITCHEN OF BETTY LEWIS)

2 eggs
¼ teaspoon salt
1 cup sugar

2 teaspoons crushed anise seed
2 cups sifted flour
1 teaspoon grated lemon zest

In large bowl, beat eggs and salt until light. Gradually beat in sugar. Continue beating until very thick and cream-colored. Add remaining ingredients. Mix well. Pour mixture onto floured surface. Knead a few times and roll or pat to ½-inch thickness. Use star-shaped cookie cutter to cut cookies. Let unbaked cookies stand overnight. Bake on greased cookie sheet in 325-degree oven for about 20 minutes. Do not allow to brown. Store in airtight container for at least 1 week before serving. Makes about 2½ dozen. Perfect for dunking in milk or coffee. If softer cookies are desired, place a few apple slices in airtight container.

Cinnamon-Sugar Butter Cookies

1 tablespoon cinnamon
½ cup plus 3 tablespoons sugar
1 cup butter, softened
1 cup packed dark brown sugar
2 large eggs

2 teaspoons vanilla
2½ cups flour
½ teaspoon baking soda
¼ teaspoon salt

Preheat oven to 300 degrees. Mix cinnamon and 3 tablespoons sugar and set aside. In bowl, beat butter, brown sugar, and ½ cup sugar; add eggs and vanilla until light and fluffy. In separate bowl, mix together flour, baking soda, and salt. Add dry ingredients to butter mixture until well combined. Don't over-mix. Shape dough into 1-inch balls and roll in cinnamon-sugar mixture. Place balls on ungreased cookie sheet. Bake for 18 to 20 minutes. Makes 3 dozen.

Pumpkin Chocolate Chip Cookies

(FROM THE KITCHEN OF AMANDA MUNRO)

1 cup shortening or margarine
2 cups sugar
2 eggs
2 teaspoons vanilla
2 tablespoons milk
1 (15 ounce) can pumpkin

2 teaspoons baking powder
2 teaspoons baking soda
1 teaspoon salt
1 teaspoon cinnamon
3½ cups flour

Preheat oven to 400 degrees. In bowl, cream shortening and sugar. Add eggs, vanilla, milk, and pumpkin. In another bowl, mix baking powder, baking soda, salt, cinnamon, and flour. Combine wet and dry ingredients and mix well. Stir in chocolate chips. Drop by teaspoonfuls onto ungreased cookie sheet. Bake for 10 minutes.

Saltine Chocolate

(FROM THE KITCHEN OF DAWN CARROLL)

1 sleeve saltine crackers
1 cup butter (do not substitute)
½ cup sugar
1 (12 ounce) package chocolate chips

Chocolate toffee bar (optional)
Candy cane pieces (optional)

Preheat oven to 350 degrees. Spread crackers in single layer on rimmed cookie sheet. Melt butter with sugar until just starting to boil and pour over saltines. Spread butter and sugar mixture gently over crackers. Bake for 5 minutes. Top with chocolate chips and return to oven for 1 minute. Spread melted chocolate chips evenly across crackers. Sprinkle crushed chocolate toffee bar or candy cane on top if desired. Freeze for 20 minutes. Break into pieces.

Grandpa's Figgy Cookies

(FROM THE KITCHEN OF SARAH REID)

Filling:
⅔ cup diced dried figs
⅓ cup grape or orange juice
⅓ cup unsweetened applesauce
4 teaspoons lemon juice
2 teaspoons cinnamon

Dough:
⅓ cup flour
¾ cup whole wheat flour
¼ cup brown sugar
¼ teaspoon baking powder
¼ teaspoon baking soda
¼ teaspoon cinnamon
¼ teaspoon salt
⅓ cup shortening
1 egg
1 egg yolk
1 egg white mixed with 2
    tablespoons water for egg wash

In small saucepan, combine all filling ingredients and bring to a simmer. Simmer until figs absorb all liquid, about 15 minutes. Let cool. Puree in food processor before chilling completely. In bowl, combine flours, sugar, baking powder, baking soda, cinnamon, and salt. Cut in shortening until dough is coarse, mealy texture. Add whole egg and egg yolk and blend in until dough comes together. Shape into disk, wrap, and chill for 1 hour. Preheat oven to 375 degrees. On lightly floured surface, roll out dough into rectangle just under ¼ inch thick. Using knife or pastry cutter, cut strips of dough about 5 inches wide. Spoon filling along center of each strip. Don't overfill! Brush one side of pastry dough with egg wash and fold other side of pastry over filling so that egg-washed side meets it. Trim edges. Transfer filled cookie tube to greased or lined baking sheet and press down to flatten slightly. Repeat with remaining strips. Brush tops with egg wash. Bake for 15 to 18 minutes until a light golden brown. Cool cookies on sheets before cutting into slices.

Holiday Candy Fudge Bars

(FROM THE KITCHEN OF KRISTINA ANDERSON)

2 cups uncooked quick oats
1½ cups flour
1 cup chopped pecans
1 cup packed light brown sugar
1 teaspoon baking soda
¼ teaspoon salt
1 cup butter or margarine, melted
1½ cups red and white candy-coated chocolate pieces, divided
1 (14 ounce) can sweetened condensed milk

Preheat oven to 375 degrees. In large bowl, combine oats, flour, pecans, brown sugar, baking soda, and salt, stirring well. Add butter and beat at low speed until mixture is crumbly. Reserve 1½ cups crumb mixture; press remaining crumb mixture into lightly greased 9x13-inch pan. Bake for 10 minutes. Cool on wire rack. Reduce oven temperature to 350 degrees. In microwave-safe bowl, microwave 1 cup candy-coated chocolate pieces on high for 1 to 1½ minutes, stirring after 30 seconds. Press chocolate pieces with back of spoon to mash them (candies will be almost melted with pieces of color coating still visible). Stir in condensed milk. Spread evenly over crust in pan, leaving ½-inch border on all sides. Combine reserved 1½ cups crumb mixture and remaining ½ cup candy-coated chocolate pieces; sprinkle evenly over chocolate mixture and press lightly. Bake at 350 degrees for 25 to 28 minutes or until golden; cool in pan on wire rack. Cut into bars.

Cranberry Nut Bread

2 cups flour
½ cup sugar
1½ teaspoons baking powder
½ teaspoon baking soda
½ teaspoon salt
½ cup brown sugar

¼ cup butter
1 egg
¾ cup orange juice
1½ cups chopped
   fresh cranberries
1 cup chopped pecans

Preheat oven to 350 degrees. Grease and lightly flour standard-sized loaf pan or three 3x5-inch loaf pans. In large bowl, sift together flour, sugar, baking powder, baking soda, and salt. Add brown sugar and mix well. Cut in butter using pastry blender until very coarse crumbs are formed. In separate bowl, stir together egg and orange juice. Gradually stir into flour mixture until flour is moistened. Gently fold in cranberries and pecans. Pour batter into prepared pan. Bake for 65 minutes (45 minutes if using smaller pans) or until toothpick comes out clean. Place pan on wire rack. Allow to cool for 10 minutes. Turn bread out carefully onto wire rack and allow to cool completely.

Frosty Desserts

Perhaps the best Yuletide decoration
is being wreathed in smiles.

UNKNOWN

Frozen Fruit Cake

1 (16 ounce) can cranberry sauce, stirred
1 cup miniature marshmallows
½ cup sugar
1 (20 ounce) can crushed pineapple, drained
½ cup chopped nuts
2 bananas, mashed

Mix all ingredients and pour into oblong pan or mold. Freeze, cut, and serve.

Unbaked Alaska

1 prepared angel food cake
1 pint orange sherbet
1 pint lime sherbet
1 container whipped topping

Divide angel food cake into 3 layers. Place first layer on serving plate. Cover with orange sherbet. Place second layer on top of sherbet. Cover second layer with lime sherbet. Place final layer on top of sherbet. Cover entire cake with whipped topping. Place in freezer until set (approximately 2 hours) or ready to serve. Remove from freezer and serve immediately.

Snow Ice Cream

5 cups freshly fallen clean snow (unpacked)
1 cup half-and-half
½ cup sugar
½ teaspoon vanilla

Place snow in freezer until ready to use. Mix half-and-half, sugar, and vanilla until blended and sugar is dissolved. Remove snow from freezer and add to cream mixture. Stir until blended and serve immediately.

Cranberry Milkshake

5½ ounces cranberry juice
½ cup vanilla ice cream
8 ounces plain yogurt

Place all ingredients in blender. Cover. Blend at high speed for 30 seconds or until creamy smooth. Makes 2 servings.

Peppermint Ice Cream

¾ cup whole milk, chilled
⅔ cup sugar
1 cup light cream
½ cup whipping cream
1 teaspoon peppermint extract

Using hand mixer or whisk, combine milk and sugar in bowl. Stir until sugar is dissolved, 1 to 2 minutes. Stir in creams and extract. Follow ice cream machine instructions.

Peppermint Milkshake

1½ cups Peppermint Ice Cream (see page 98)
¾ cup milk
Green or red food coloring

Put all ingredients in blender and blend on high speed for about 30 seconds until mixed well. Makes 2 servings.

After-Dinner Ice Cream

¾ cup whole milk, chilled
⅔ cup sugar
1 cup light cream
½ cup whipping cream
1 teaspoon peppermint extract
1 package after-dinner chocolate-covered mints

Using hand mixer or whisk, combine milk and sugar in bowl. Stir until sugar is dissolved, 1 to 2 minutes. Stir in creams and extract. Follow ice cream machine instructions. Chop after-dinner mints into small pieces. About 5 minutes before ice cream is done, add desired amount of mint pieces.

Eggnog Ice Cream

¾ cup Eggnog (see page 18), chilled
⅓ cup sugar
1 cup heavy cream
½ cup whole milk

Using hand mixer or whisk, combine eggnog and sugar in bowl. Stir until sugar is dissolved, 1 to 2 minutes. Stir in cream and milk. Follow ice cream machine instructions.

Eggnog Milkshake

1½ cups Eggnog Ice Cream (see page 101)
¾ cup milk
Pinch nutmeg

Put all ingredients in blender and blend on high speed for about 30 seconds until mixed well. Pour into cups and sprinkle with nutmeg. Makes 2 servings.

Gingerbread Milkshake

1½ cups Eggnog Ice Cream (see page 101)
¾ cup milk
1 gingerbread cookie
Pinch allspice

Put all ingredients in blender and blend on high speed for about 30 seconds until mixed well. Pour into cups and sprinkle with allspice. Makes 2 servings.

Frosty Strawberry Squares

1 cup flour
½ cup butter or margarine
¼ cup brown sugar
½ cup chopped walnuts
⅔ cup sugar

2 egg whites
1 (10 ounce) package frozen
    strawberries, partially thawed
2 tablespoons lemon juice
½ pint whipping cream, whipped

Preheat oven to 350 degrees. In bowl, mix flour, butter, brown sugar, and walnuts. Press into ungreased 9x13-inch pan and bake for 20 minutes, stirring occasionally. Let cool. Remove one-third of crust mix from pan and reserve. Beat sugar, egg whites, strawberries, and lemon juice until mixed. Beat on high speed for 10 to 15 minutes. Mixture will become very stiff. Fold whipped cream into strawberry mixture. Pour over crust. Sprinkle reserved topping over dessert. Freeze until set. Cut into squares to serve.

Traditional Desserts

I will honor Christmas in my heart,
and try to keep it all the year.

CHARLES DICKENS

Russian Tea Cakes

1 cup butter, softened
½ cup powdered sugar, sifted
1 teaspoon vanilla
2¼ cups flour, sifted
¼ teaspoon salt
¾ cup finely chopped pecans or walnuts

In bowl, mix butter, powdered sugar, and vanilla. In separate bowl, combine flour and salt. Blend flour mixture with butter mixture. Stir in nuts. Chill for 1 hour. Preheat oven to 400 degrees. Roll dough into 1-inch balls and place on ungreased baking sheet. Bake for 10 to 12 minutes until set but not browned. While still warm, roll in powdered sugar and let cool.

Red Velvet Cake

4 tablespoons cocoa
1 ounce red food coloring
¾ cup water, divided
1 box pudding cake mix (white or yellow)
4 eggs

1 teaspoon vanilla
1 teaspoon butter flavoring
4 tablespoons buttermilk powder
1 tablespoon white vinegar

Preheat oven to 325 degrees. In large bowl, mix cocoa, red food coloring, and small amount of water to form paste. Add cake mix, eggs, vanilla, butter flavoring, and buttermilk powder. Mix for 3 minutes on medium speed until well blended. Add vinegar and blend completely. Pour batter into greased 9x13-inch cake pan and bake for 35 minutes or until toothpick inserted in center comes out clean. Frost with Boiled Frosting (see page 108).

Boiled Frosting

4½ cups sugar
1¼ cups hot water
4 egg whites
1 tablespoon vanilla

In large saucepan, combine sugar and water and cook over medium-high heat. Stir until sugar is dissolved. Boil without stirring to soft ball stage (238 degrees). Beat egg whites on high speed until stiff but not dry. Gradually pour syrup over egg whites while beating. Continue beating until icing is spreadable. Add vanilla. Spread on cake immediately.

Amaretti

2 egg whites
¼ teaspoon salt
1 cup sugar
1 cup chopped blanched almonds
¾ teaspoon almond extract

Add salt to egg whites and beat until frothy. Add sugar gradually, beating until mixture is stiff but not dry. Add almonds and almond extract and fold in gently. Drop almond mixture by teaspoonfuls onto greased and floured baking sheet. Shape into small mounds, leaving room between each mound. Let stand 2 hours. Bake at 375 degrees for 12 minutes or until delicately brown in color.

Cranberry Cake

4 tablespoons butter
2 cups sugar
4 cups flour
6 teaspoons baking powder
Pinch salt
2 cups milk, divided
2 teaspoons vanilla
3 cups fresh cranberries

Sauce:
1 cup butter
2 cups sugar
1½ cups cream

Preheat oven to 350 degrees. Grease and flour 9x13-inch pan. In large bowl, cream butter and sugar. In separate bowl, mix dry ingredients. Add one-third of dry ingredients to butter-sugar mixture. Then add ⅔ cup milk. Continue alternating dry ingredients and milk until all are added. Add vanilla and cranberries. Pour into prepared pan. Bake for 30 minutes or until toothpick comes out clean.

Sauce: Brown butter in large saucepan over medium heat, stirring constantly. Add sugar and cream and boil for 1 minute. To serve, spoon sauce over each slice.

Jesus' Birthday Cake

(FROM THE KITCHEN OF BETTY LEWIS)

1 box chocolate fudge cake mix
1 box instant chocolate pudding mix
¾ cup plus 2 tablespoons water
4 eggs
¼ cup oil
1 ounce red food coloring

Frosting:
1 package buttercream fudge
 frosting mix
1½ cups sour cream
½ cup chopped walnuts

Preheat oven to 350 degrees. Combine all cake ingredients in mixing bowl. Blend thoroughly. Beat at medium speed for 8 minutes. Turn batter into generously greased and lightly floured 9x13-inch cake pan or 2 round cake pans. Bake for 40 to 45 minutes or until toothpick comes out clean. Cool cake in pan for 15 minutes before frosting.

Frosting: Combine frosting mix and sour cream. Blend just until smooth. Spread on warm cake and sprinkle with nuts. Return to 350-degree oven for 10 minutes to set frosting.

Remarkable Fudge

4 cups sugar
2 (5 ounce) cans evaporated milk
1 cup butter
1 (7 ounce) jar marshmallow crème

1 cup milk chocolate chips
1 teaspoon vanilla
1 cup chopped nuts (optional)
2 cups semisweet chocolate chips

Line 9x13-inch baking pan with foil, extending foil over edges of pan. Butter foil; set pan aside. Butter sides of large, heavy saucepan. Combine sugar, milk, and butter in saucepan. Cook and stir over medium-high heat until mixture boils. Reduce heat to medium; continue cooking for 10 minutes, stirring constantly. Remove pan from heat. Add remaining ingredients and stir until chocolate melts. Beat by hand for 1 minute. Spread in prepared pan. Score into 1-inch pieces while still warm. When fudge is firm, use foil to lift out of pan. Cut fudge into squares. Store in tightly covered container in refrigerator. Makes about 3 pounds.

Mexican Wedding Cookies

1 cup butter
1 cup powdered sugar, divided
1½ teaspoons vanilla
2 cups sifted flour
1 cup chopped nuts

Preheat oven to 325 degrees. In bowl, cream butter, ¾ cup powdered sugar, and vanilla. Add flour and nuts gradually. Mix until blended. Form into 1-inch balls. Bake for 25 minutes. Roll immediately in remaining ¼ cup sugar. Allow to cool and roll in sugar again.

Christmas Povatica

(A Traditional Eastern European Christmas Dessert from the Kitchen of the Bahun Family)

Pastry dough:
4 cups flour
3 tablespoons sugar
1½ teaspoons salt
½ cup butter
1 package yeast
¼ cup lukewarm water
1 teaspoon sugar
3 egg yolks, beaten
1 cup cream

Filling:
1¼ pounds walnuts, ground
1 cup scalded milk
½ cup butter
1 cup sugar
4 egg whites, stiffly beaten
1 egg yolk, for brushing before baking
Grated lemon zest (optional)

In bowl, sift flour, 3 tablespoons sugar, and salt. Cut in butter. Dissolve yeast in lukewarm water; add 1 teaspoon sugar. Let stand until foamy. Add egg yolks and cream. Make dent in flour and add yeast mixture. Knead into smooth dough. Place in bowl and grease top. For filling, pour scalded milk over ground nuts. Add butter and stir until melted. Add sugar and egg whites. Refrigerate filling and pastry dough overnight.

Next day: Remove pastry dough from refrigerator and leave on counter for 30 minutes. Dust surface with flour and turn dough out on surface. Roll dough very thin with rolling pin, continuing to flour work surface and dough surface as needed. Roll out in large circle. Spread with refrigerated filling and lemon zest. Roll up dough and filling and place on greased jelly roll pan or large cookie sheet. Form ends into crescent shape. Let rise for at least 90 minutes. Brush egg yolk on top and bake for 60 to 75 minutes at 325 degrees. Loaf may split in a few places while baking.

Chocolate Buttermilk Cake

(FROM THE KITCHEN OF BARBARA PINKHAM)

2 cups sugar
1¾ cups flour
¾ cup cocoa
2 teaspoons baking soda
1 teaspoon baking powder
1 teaspoon salt

2 eggs
1 cup brewed coffee
1 cup buttermilk
½ cup oil
1 teaspoon vanilla

Preheat oven to 350 degrees. Grease 2 round cake pans. In bowl, combine sugar, flour, cocoa, baking soda, baking powder, and salt and mix well. Add eggs, coffee, buttermilk, oil, and vanilla and mix. Pour into prepared pans. Bake for about 28 minutes or until toothpick inserted in center comes out clean. Let cool for 15 minutes in pans and remove to wire rack to finish cooling. Once cool, frost with Chocolate Cream Cheese Frosting (see page 119).

Chocolate Cream Cheese Frosting

(FROM THE KITCHEN OF BARBARA PINKHAM)

5 tablespoons butter
4 ounces cream cheese, softened
¼ cup milk
½ cup cocoa
3 cups powdered sugar
1 teaspoon vanilla
½ teaspoon espresso powder

Beat all ingredients together until smooth.

Spice Cake

(FROM THE KITCHEN OF JAIE'S GRAMMY)

2 cups buttermilk
2 teaspoons baking soda
1 teaspoon vanilla
1 cup shortening
1 teaspoon salt
2 cups sugar

3 eggs
1 tablespoon cocoa
1 teaspoon allspice
1 teaspoon cinnamon
¼ teaspoon nutmeg
3 cups sifted flour

Preheat oven to 350 degrees. In bowl, combine buttermilk, baking soda, and vanilla. Let stand. In separate bowl, beat shortening, salt, sugar, and eggs until creamy. In third bowl, sift together cocoa, allspice, cinnamon, and nutmeg. Combine sifted spices with sifted flour. Flour must be sifted. To bowl with creamed shortening-sugar mixture, gradually add flour and spice mixture and buttermilk mixture. Add 1 spoonful of flour then a little of buttermilk mixture. Always end with buttermilk mixture. Beat until smooth. Bake for 35 to 40 minutes in two 9-inch round cake pans that have been greased and floured. Cool. Frost with Cream Cheese Frosting (see page 122).

Cream Cheese Frosting

1 (8 ounce) package cream cheese, softened
½ cup butter
1 pound powdered sugar
1 to 3 tablespoons milk
1 teaspoon flavoring extract (vanilla, almond, rum, etc.)

With electric mixer, beat cream cheese and butter until smooth. Add powdered sugar and milk gradually until desired frosting reaches consistency. Stir in flavoring and spread on cake.

Mom's Christmas Shortbread

(FROM THE KITCHEN OF SARAH REID)

1 cup unsalted butter, softened
1 egg yolk
1 teaspoon vanilla
½ cup powdered sugar

2 cups flour
Christmas sprinkles
Colored sugar
Chocolate chips

Preheat oven to 325 degrees. In bowl, cream butter, egg yolk, and vanilla. Sift powdered sugar and flour into creamed mixture. Mix to form workable dough. Roll out and cut into shapes with cookie cutters. Place cookies on ungreased cookie sheets. Decorate with sprinkles, colored sugar, or chocolate chips, or leave plain. Bake for 20 minutes. Cookies should not brown. Let cool completely on sheets. Store in airtight container.

Rum Cake

2 cups sugar
1 cup shortening
2 tablespoons rum extract
2 cups buttermilk
4 cups flour
2 teaspoons baking soda

¼ teaspoon salt
¼ teaspoon ground cloves
¼ teaspoon cinnamon
¼ teaspoon nutmeg
2 cups raisins or dried cranberries

Preheat oven to 350 degrees. Grease and flour 9x13-inch pan. In large bowl, cream sugar and shortening. Mix in rum extract. Sift together dry ingredients and add alternately with buttermilk to creamed mixture. Fold in dried fruit. Pour into prepared pan. Bake for 45 to 50 minutes. Frost with Boiled Frosting (see page 108) or Cream Cheese Frosting (see page 122).

Almond Lace Cookies

¾ cup finely chopped almonds
½ cup sugar
½ cup butter

1 tablespoon flour
2 tablespoons milk
1 teaspoon grated lemon zest

Preheat oven to 350 degrees. Grease and flour 2 cookie sheets. In large saucepan, combine all ingredients. Stir over low heat with wooden spoon until butter is melted and ingredients are well mixed. Remove from heat. Place heaping teaspoons of batter on cookie sheets about 5 inches apart. Batter will spread during baking. Bake for 9 to 10 minutes or until evenly browned. Allow to cool on sheets for about 5 minutes to set in flat shape or, using wide spatula, remove cookies from sheets and immediately shape into tightly rolled tubes or fans. Store in airtight containers for a couple of days or in freezer for up to 3 weeks.

Pfefferneuse (German Christmas Cookies)

½ cup molasses
¼ cup sugar
¼ cup shortening
1 egg, beaten
2¼ cups flour

½ teaspoon baking soda
¼ teaspoon ground cloves
¼ teaspoon nutmeg
¼ teaspoon cinnamon
Powdered sugar (optional)

Preheat oven to 375 degrees. In saucepan, combine molasses, sugar, and shortening; cook and stir until shortening and sugar melt. Cool. Stir in egg. In separate bowl, mix flour with soda and spices. Add to molasses mixture and mix well. Form into balls using 1 level tablespoon dough for each. Place on greased cookie sheet. Bake for about 10 minutes. Cool. If desired, sift powdered sugar over tops.

Eggnog Pie

(From the Kitchen of Caren Blasi)

2 teaspoons unflavored gelatin
½ cup sugar
2 tablespoons cornstarch
¼ teaspoon salt
1 cup milk

3 egg yolks, beaten
1½ teaspoons vanilla
1 cup heavy cream, whipped
1 prebaked piecrust
Nutmeg for garnish

In saucepan, blend first 4 ingredients. Stir in milk gradually. Cook over medium heat, stirring constantly until mixture thickens and boils. Boil for 1 minute. Remove from heat. Stir in egg yolks. Return to heat. Bring just to boiling. Remove from heat. Add vanilla and let cool until mixture mounds slightly when dropped from spoon. Fold in whipped cream. Pour into piecrust and sprinkle with nutmeg. Keep refrigerated.

Cherry Mincemeat Pies

(FROM THE KITCHEN OF BARBARA BAHUN)

Pastry for two 2-crust, 9-inch pies
2 cups prepared mincemeat
1 (21 ounce) can cherry pie filling
½ cup orange marmalade
1 tablespoon whole wheat flour
¼ cup chopped walnuts

Preheat oven to 400 degrees. Line two 9-inch pie plates with pastry. In bowl, combine mincemeat, cherry pie filling, orange marmalade, flour, and nuts. Divide between two pastry shells. Top each with lattice crust; trim and flute edges. Bake for 35 to 40 minutes.

Basic Sugar Cookies

2 cups salted butter, softened
1½ cups sugar
2 large eggs

2 teaspoons vanilla
½ teaspoon salt
5 cups flour

In large bowl, cream butter and sugar. Beat in eggs until evenly mixed. Add vanilla and salt. With wooden spoon, stir flour into butter mixture, adding flour gradually. Dough may be soft but will firm up when refrigerated. Divide dough into 4 pieces and flatten into disks. Cover in plastic wrap and refrigerate for at least 1 hour. Remove from refrigerator and roll out to ½-inch thickness. Cut out cookies with large Christmas cookie cutters. Arrange on cookie sheet and bake at 375 degrees for 8 to 10 minutes. Let cookies cool for a few minutes on cookie sheet and then transfer to wire rack. When completely cooled, frost with Basic Cookie Icing (see page 130).

Basic Cookie Icing

4 cups powdered sugar
4 tablespoons butter, softened
3 to 5 tablespoons milk
Red and green food coloring (optional)

Blend all ingredients until smooth. Add food coloring if desired.

Rum Balls

⅓ cup water
2 teaspoons rum extract
2½ tablespoons light corn syrup
2½ cups crushed vanilla wafers
1 cup finely chopped pecans

½ cup sugar
Dash salt
1½ tablespoons cocoa
1 cup powdered sugar

Mix together water, rum extract, and corn syrup. Add vanilla wafers, pecans, sugar, salt, and cocoa. Mix thoroughly and form into small balls. Roll in powdered sugar and store in tin lined with waxed paper.

Norwegian Christmas Cookies

(FROM THE KITCHEN OF LAURA M.)

1½ cups shortening
1½ cups sugar
1 egg yolk
1 whole egg
2½ cups flour

½ teaspoon ground cardamom
½ teaspoon cinnamon
1 cup ground blanched almonds
1 tablespoon orange juice

In bowl, cream shortening and sugar and add egg yolk and whole egg. In separate bowl, mix dry ingredients and almonds. Combine mixtures and add orange juice. Chill dough; then roll thin, cut in fancy shapes, and bake for 5 to 7 minutes at 400 degrees. Cookies must be watched carefully to avoid overbaking.

Eggnog Fudge

2 cups sugar
1 cup Eggnog (see page 18)
1 tablespoon light corn syrup
2 tablespoons butter
1 teaspoon vanilla
½ cup finely chopped pecans

Butter sides of heavy saucepan. In pan, combine sugar, eggnog, and corn syrup. Cook over medium heat, stirring constantly until sugar dissolves and mixture comes to a boil. Cook to soft ball stage (238 degrees), stirring occasionally. Immediately remove from heat and cool to lukewarm (98 degrees) without stirring. Add butter and vanilla. Beat vigorously until fudge becomes very thick and starts to lose its gloss. Mix in pecans quickly. Spread in buttered 8x8-inch pan.

Linzer Torte

½ cup plus 1 tablespoon sugar
1 cup flour
½ teaspoon cinnamon
⅛ teaspoon ground cloves
½ cup butter

1 cup ground almonds
½ to 1 teaspoon lemon zest
1 egg plus 1 yolk
1 (12 ounce) jar raspberry jam

Combine dry ingredients; then cut in butter. Stir in almonds and lemon zest. Add eggs. Refrigerate for easy handling. Roll out two-thirds of mixture and put in 8-inch pie pan. Spread with jam. Roll remainder and cut into strips. Make lattice crust over jam. Bake at 350 degrees for about 45 minutes.

Pepparkakor (Swedish Christmas Gingersnaps)

2 tablespoons water
2 tablespoons syrup (golden syrup is best)
5½ tablespoons butter or margarine
2 cups flour
½ cup plus 2 tablespoons sugar

½ tablespoon baking soda
½ teaspoon ginger
½ teaspoon cinnamon
½ teaspoon ground cloves

In saucepan, heat water and syrup. Pour over butter in large bowl. Sift dry ingredients and combine with syrup-margarine mixture. Refrigerate overnight. Roll out very thin and cut with Christmas cookie cutters. Bake at 350 degrees on greased cookie sheet for about 10 minutes.

Basic Pumpkin Pie

1 unbaked 9-inch piecrust
¾ cup sugar
½ teaspoon salt
1 teaspoon cinnamon
½ teaspoon ground ginger

¼ teaspoon ground cloves
¼ teaspoon ground nutmeg
2 eggs
1 (15 ounce) can pumpkin
1 (12 ounce) can evaporated
  milk

Preheat oven to 425 degrees. Put piecrust into pie pan. Trim edges and save excess pie dough for decorating. In small bowl, mix sugar and spices together. In large bowl, beat eggs and stir in pumpkin and spice mixture. Gradually stir in evaporated milk. Pour into piecrust. Bake for 15 minutes. Roll out excess pie dough on cutting board. Using Christmas cookie cutters, cut out 3 or 4 shapes. Place shapes on top of pie in oven. Reduce temperature to 350 degrees. Bake for 40 to 50 minutes or until knife inserted in center comes out clean. Place on wire rack until cool. Serve immediately or refrigerate.

Holiday Dump Cake

1 (21 ounce) can cherry pie filling
1 (20 ounce) can crushed pineapple
1 yellow cake mix with pudding

½ cup butter, melted
Christmas sprinkles

Preheat oven to 350 degrees. Dump cherry pie filling and crushed pineapple into 8x8-inch ungreased cake pan. Mix together. Dump cake mix evenly over the cherry mixture. Pour melted butter evenly over cake mix. Generously sprinkle with Christmas sprinkles. Bake for about 35 minutes or until cherry mixture bubbles around edges and top of cake mixture is hard.

Cream Candy

(FROM THE KITCHEN OF GLADYS ROBERTS)

6 tablespoons butter, divided
½ cup sugar
½ cup light corn syrup

½ cup milk
1 teaspoon vanilla
1 heaping cup pecans

Toast the pecans with half the butter, salting slightly. In large, heavy-bottomed saucepan, combine sugar, corn syrup, milk, and remaining butter. Bring to rolling boil and boil for 3 minutes. Remove from heat and add vanilla and pecans. Beat with wooden spoon until mixture becomes pliable and cools down significantly. Drop by spoonfuls onto waxed paper to harden.

Swedish Cranberry Apple Pie

(FROM THE KITCHEN OF SANDY JOHNSON)

Cranberries (fresh or frozen)
Tart apples
1 cup plus 3 teaspoons sugar, divided
1 teaspoon cinnamon
1 cup flour

1 egg
⅔ cup butter or margarine, softened
½ cup coarsely chopped walnuts

Preheat oven to 350 degrees. Line bottom of empty pie pan with one layer of cranberries. Peel and slice apples on top of cranberries until dish is two-thirds full. Sprinkle apples with mixture of 3 teaspoons sugar and cinnamon. In a bowl, combine flour, 1 cup sugar, egg, butter, and walnuts. Spread stiff batter over apples. Bake for 45 minutes.

Gingersnaps

¾ cup butter, softened
⅔ cup sugar
⅔ cup packed dark brown sugar
1 egg
2 cups flour

1 tablespoon ginger
1 teaspoon cinnamon
2 teaspoons baking soda
½ teaspoon salt
Sugar

Preheat oven to 350 degrees. In medium bowl, cream butter and sugars until smooth. Beat in egg until well blended. Combine remaining ingredients. Add to butter mixture to form dough. Roll dough into 1-inch balls and roll balls in shallow bowl of sugar. Place cookies 2 inches apart on ungreased cookie sheets. Bake for 7 to 9 minutes. Let cookies cool on sheets for a few minutes before removing to wire rack to cool completely.

Coconut Macaroons

6 large egg whites
1½ cups sugar
½ teaspoon salt
1 teaspoon vanilla

1 cup sifted flour
3½ cups sweetened coconut
½ teaspoon almond or rum
extract

Heat saucepan of water to soft boil. Place stainless steel or heatproof bowl over pan and whisk egg whites, sugar, and salt. When mixture is lukewarm, remove from heat and add vanilla, flour, coconut, and extract. Cover bowl and chill until dough is firm (about 90 minutes). Preheat oven to 325 degrees and line 2 cookie sheets with parchment paper. Use 2 tablespoons to drop cookies on sheets, spacing well apart. Bake for 15 minutes or until golden. Remove from oven and leave on sheets for 8 minutes before removing to wire rack to cool completely. Makes about 3 dozen.

Fruitcake

3 cups sifted flour
2 teaspoons baking powder
1 teaspoon salt
2 teaspoons cinnamon
½ teaspoon nutmeg
½ teaspoon ground cloves
½ teaspoon ginger
3 cups raisins
1½ cups chopped dates
4½ cups candied fruits (cherries, pineapple,
    apricots, lemons, orange peel)

1 cup chopped pecans
1 cup slivered almonds
4 eggs
1¾ cups brown sugar
1 cup orange juice
¼ cup molasses
¾ cup butter, melted but
    not hot

Preheat oven to 300 degrees. Line two 4x8-inch loaf pans with waxed paper and grease. In large bowl, mix dry ingredients. Add fruits and nuts, mixing until well coated with dry ingredients. In separate bowl, beat eggs until frothy and gradually add brown sugar. Mix in orange juice, molasses, and butter. Add to fruit mixture and stir until thoroughly mixed. Pour batter into prepared loaf pans, filling each three-quarters full. Bake for approximately 2 hours. Cool thoroughly before removing from pans.

Buche de Noel

1 cup plus 2 tablespoons sugar
2 (1 ounce) packages liquid
  unsweetened chocolate
3 tablespoons cold water
1½ teaspoons vanilla, divided
¼ teaspoon baking soda
4 eggs
½ cup sifted flour
½ teaspoon baking powder

½ teaspoon salt
1 cup heavy cream
¼ cup each chopped walnuts
  and candied orange peel
Flaked coconut
Green food coloring
Basic Chocolate Frosting (see
  page 147)

Preheat oven to 375 degrees. Grease 10x15x1-inch pan, line with waxed paper, and grease again. Mix 2 tablespoons sugar, chocolate, water, 1 teaspoon vanilla, and baking soda until thick and smooth; set aside. Beat eggs until foamy. Gradually add 1 cup sugar and beat until very thick and lemon-colored. Fold in sifted flour, baking powder, and salt. Then quickly fold in chocolate mixture and spread in prepared pan. Bake for 15 to 18 minutes or until toothpick comes out clean. Do not overbake.

Carefully loosen edges and invert cake on towel sprinkled with powdered sugar. Remove paper and trim off crisp edges. Cool for 5 minutes; then roll up in towel and put on wire rack. Cool thoroughly.

Whip cream and fold in walnuts, orange peel, and ½ teaspoon vanilla. Unroll cake and spread with cream mixture. Reroll, wrap in towel, and chill. Tint coconut green with a little food coloring rubbed in with fingertips. Spread top, sides, and ends of roll with chocolate frosting and sprinkle with coconut.

Buche de Noel (Shortcuts)

Substitute a container of whipped topping mixed with 1 tablespoon cocoa for the filling. Spread over prepared cake and roll per traditional recipe.

Use premade chocolate frosting instead of homemade frosting. An alternate garnish would be sprinkling the top with Christmas sprinkles or store-bought holly branches.

Basic Chocolate Frosting

¼ cup butter, softened
2 (1 ounce) packages liquid unsweetened chocolate
3 cups powdered sugar
⅓ cup milk
1 teaspoon vanilla

Cream butter with chocolate. Gradually blend in sugar alternately with milk and vanilla.

Spicy Plum Pie

5 cups plum slices	½ teaspoon ginger
½ cup sugar	¼ teaspoon salt
¼ cup packed brown sugar	2 tablespoons butter
3 tablespoons cornstarch	Pastry for two 9-inch piecrusts
½ teaspoon cinnamon	Ice cream or whipped cream for topping

Preheat oven to 425 degrees. Toss fruit with sugars, cornstarch, cinnamon, ginger, and salt until well covered. Line 9-inch pie pan with pastry. Spoon plum mixture into pastry shell. Dot with butter. Roll remaining pastry into 11-inch circle and cut into 1-inch strips. Weave lattice top over pie. Seal edges and flute with fork. Bake for 45 to 50 minutes; cover edges with pie shield or foil during last 20 minutes. Serve with ice cream or whipped cream.

Gingerbread People

½ cup butter
½ cup sugar
½ cup molasses
¼ cup water
2¼ cups flour
1 teaspoon salt

½ teaspoon baking soda
½ teaspoon ginger
½ teaspoon allspice
Basic Cookie Icing (see page 130)
Raisins, candied fruit, gum
   drops, candied corn, and string
   licorice for decorating

In large bowl, cream butter and sugar. Mix in molasses, water, flour, salt, baking soda, ginger, and allspice. Chill for at least 3 hours. Preheat oven to 375 degrees. Cover work surface with parchment paper and lightly flour. Roll dough to ½-inch thickness. Cut with cookie cutters. Bake on ungreased cookie sheet for 10 minutes. Immediately remove from cookie sheet and cool. Decorate Gingerbread People with icing, raisins, and candy.

Gingerbread House
(Inedible—For Display Only)

Mix up a double batch of Gingerbread People recipe (see page 149). Patterns for cutting out gingerbread house are available through an Internet search for "gingerbread house pattern." Cut out pieces before baking. While pieces are in oven, cover a place mat–sized piece of plywood with heavy-duty aluminum foil. Prepare Royal Icing (see page 152) for constructing and decorating house.

Once gingerbread pieces are removed from oven, allow to cool completely on wire racks. Begin constructing your house by piping a thick line of icing along the edges of a side wall and attach it to one of the front walls. Continue attaching each piece of the house until the structure is completed. Icing may leak out of the seams, but you can use a sharp knife to remove excess icing after it dries. Pipe lines of icing in the general shape of the bottom of your gingerbread house. Attach house to foil-covered board by pressing down firmly into icing outline. Allow to set overnight. Store remaining icing tightly covered with plastic wrap in refrigerator.

The next day, begin the process of decorating the house. Fill three pastry bags with white, red, and green icing using a small tip. Decorate house by outlining a door, windows, and roof with icing. You can also use the icing to attach gum drops, candy-coated chocolates, and other creative candies. If you plan to display the house for several days or weeks, spray with polyurethane and allow to dry completely.

Royal Icing (Inedible—For Display Only)

6 egg whites
3 pounds powdered sugar
Green and red food coloring

Beat egg whites until foamy. Gradually beat in sugar until icing is desired consistency. The more you beat the icing, the fluffier it gets. You want to use very fluffy icing to construct a gingerbread house and less fluffy icing to decorate the house. Remove one-quarter of the icing and mix in a few drops of green food coloring until desired shade. Remove another quarter of icing and mix in a few drops of red food coloring until desired shade. Place remaining white icing into a pastry bag with a small tip.